The

by Iain Gray

PUBLISHING

WRITING *to* REMEMBER

Lang**Syne**

PUBLISHING

WRITING *to* REMEMBER

Strathclyde Business Centre
120 Carstairs Street, Glasgow G40 4JD
Tel: 0141 554 9944 Fax: 0141 554 9955
E-mail: info@scottish-memories.co.uk
www.langsyneshop.co.uk

Designed by Dorothy Meikle
Printed by Thomson Litho, East Kilbride
© Lang Syne Publishers Ltd 2006
ISBN 1-85217-222-3
ISBN 978-1-85217-222-0

The Baxters

Chapter one:

Origins of Scottish surnames

by George Forbes

It all began with the Normans.

For it was they who introduced surnames into common usage more than a thousand years ago, initially based on the title of their estates, local villages and chateaux in France to distinguish and identify these landholdings, usually acquired at the point of a bloodstained sword.

Such grand descriptions also helped enhance the prestige of these arrogant warlords and generally glorify their lofty positions high above the humble serfs slaving away below in the pecking order who only had single names, often with Biblical connotations as in Pierre and Jacques.

The only descriptive distinctions

among this peasantry concerned their occupations, like Pierre the swineherd or Jacques the ferryman.

The Normans themselves were originally Vikings (or Northmen) who raided, colonised and eventually settled down around the French coastline.

They had sailed up the Seine in their longboats in 900AD under their ferocious leader Rollo and ruled the roost in north east France before sailing over to conquer England, bringing their relatively new tradition of having surnames with them.

It took another hundred years for the Normans to percolate northwards and surnames did not begin to appear in Scotland until the thirteenth century.

These adventurous knights brought an aura of chivalry with them and it was said no damsel of any distinction would marry a man unless he had at least two names.

The family names included that of Scotland's great hero Robert De Brus and his compatriots were warriors from families like the De Morevils, De Umphravils, De Berkelais, De Quincis, De Viponts and De Vaux.

As the knights settled the boundaries of their vast estates, they took territorial names, as in Hamilton, Moray, Crawford, Cunningham, Dunbar, Ross, Wemyss, Dundas, Galloway, Renfrew, Greenhill, Hazelwood, Sandylands and Church-hill.

Other names, though not with any obvious geographical or topographical features, nevertheless derived from ancient parishes like Douglas, Forbes, Dalyell and Guthrie.

Other surnames were coined in connection with occupations, castles or legendary deeds. Stuart originated in the word steward, a prestigious post which was an integral part of any large medieval household. The same applied to Cooks, Chamberlains, Constables and Porters.

Borders towns and forts - needed in

areas like the Debateable Lands which were constantly fought over by feuding local families - had their own distinctive names; and it was often from them that the resident groups took their communal titles, as in the Grahams of Annandale, the Elliots and Armstrongs of the East Marches, the Scotts and Kerrs of Teviotdale and Eskdale.

Even physical attributes crept into surnames, as in Small, Little and More (the latter being 'beg' in Gaelic), Long or Lang, Stark, Stout, Strong or Strang and even Jolly.

Mieklejohns would have had the strength of several men, while Littlejohn was named after the legendary sidekick of Robin Hood.

Colours got into the act with Black, White, Grey, Brown and Green (Red developed into Reid, Ruddy or Ruddiman). Blue was rare and nobody ever wanted to be associated with yellow.

Pompous worthies took the name Wiseman, Goodman and Goodall.

Words intimating the sons of leading figures were soon affiliated into the language as in Johnson, Adamson, Richardson and Thomson, while the Norman equivalent of Fitz (from the French-Latin 'filius' meaning 'son') cropped up in Fitzmaurice and Fitzgerald.

The prefix 'Mac' was 'son of' in Gaelic and clans often originated with occupations - as in MacNab being sons of the Abbot, MacPherson and MacVicar being sons of the minister and MacIntosh being sons of the chief.

The church's influence could be found in the names Kirk, Clerk, Clarke, Bishop, Friar and Monk. Proctor came from a church official, Singer and Sangster from choristers, Gilchrist and Gillies from Christ's servant, Mitchell, Gilmory and Gilmour from servants of St Michael and Mary, Malcolm from a servant of Columba and Gillespie from a bishop's servant.

The rudimentary medical profession was represented by Barber (a trade which also once included dentistry and surgery) as well as Leech or Leitch.

Businessmen produced Merchants, Mercers, Monypennies, Chapmans, Sellers and Scales, while down at the old village watermill the names that cropped up included Miller, Walker and Fuller.

Other self explanatory trades included Coopers, Brands, Barkers, Tanners, Skinners, Brewsters and Brewers, Tailors, Saddlers, Wrights, Cartwrights, Smiths, Harpers, Joiners, Sawyers, Masons and Plumbers.

Even the scenery was utilised as in Craig, Moor, Hill, Glen, Wood and Forrest.

Rank, whether high or low, took its place with Laird, Barron, Knight, Tennant, Farmer, Husband, Granger, Grieve, Shepherd, Shearer and Fletcher.

The hunt and the chase supplied Hunter, Falconer, Fowler, Fox, Forrester, Archer and Spearman.

The renowned medieval historian Froissart, who eulogised about the romantic deeds of chivalry (and who condemned Scotland as being a poverty stricken wasteland), once sniffily dismissed the peasantry of his native France as the jacquerie (or the jacques-without-names) but it was these same humble folk who ended up overthrowing the arrogant aristocracy.

In the olden days, only the blueblooded knights of antiquity were entitled to full, proper names, both Christian and surnames, but with the passing of time and a more egalitarian, less feudal atmosphere, more respectful and worthy titles spread throughout the populace as a whole.

Echoes of a far distant past can still be found in most names and they can be borne with pride in commemoration of past generations who fought and toiled in some capacity or other to make our nation what it now is, for good or ill.

Chapter two:

Kings of commerce

'Baxter', quite simply, is the Scottish form of the equally common English surname of 'Baker', but there is nothing common or mundane about the exploits and achievements of the generations of Baxters who have contributed, and continue to contribute, to Scotland's colourful story.

Very early records carry the name as 'Pistor', the Latin word for baker, but 'Baxter' actually derives from the Old English word 'baecestre', and the later Middle English word 'bakstere', meaning a baker.

Variations of the name include Baxtar, Bacster, Baxstare, Baxstar, and Bakster, while Scottish Gaelic forms include MacBaxtar, MacBaxter, MacBhaxter and MacBacasdar.

Originally an occupational surname, a family of Baxters are believed to have at one time served as bakers in the former royal residence at

Forfar, but not all Baxters were necessarily bakers.

The name is found throughout the length and breadth of Scotland, with a particular concentration in Fife, where it was first recorded in the early years of the thirteenth century when a Reginald Baxter witnessed a gift to the church at Wemyss.

In Forfar, meanwhile, a Jeffrey Baxtere of Lissithe is on record as having taken an oath of fealty to the ill-starred monarch John Balliol in the closing decade of the thirteenth century.

The family of Baxters who flourished in Fife even had their own family motto of 'Truth prevails', while their crest was a lion rampant – a motto and crest proudly displayed today by the hundreds of Baxters across the world who seek to maintain the rich heritage attached to the name.

A powerful family, known as the Baxters of Kincaldrum, was responsible for bringing power weaving to the city of Dundee in the early years of the industrial revolution that transformed both the physical and the social landscape of Britain.

Along with the Baxters of Balgavies, the

family was associated with the famous Baxter Brothers and Company, whose products not only found lucrative markets in the farthest corners of the globe, but who also had the distinction of supplying the sails for the entire British naval fleet that won victory for Admiral Nelson at the battle of Trafalgar, in 1805.

The Baxters of Kincaldrum literally left their mark on Dundee, in the form of land they gifted and now known as Baxter Park, while a college they endowed is now the centre of academic excellence known as the University of Dundee.

In Morayshire, a family of Baxters has thrived for nearly 140 years at Fochabers, on the River Spey, as purveyors of fine foodstuffs made from local produce.

In its fourth generation, what has now become the Baxters Food Group was born in 1868 when George Baxter, a gardener at Gordon Castle, the home of the Duke of Richmond and Gordon, borrowed £100 from relatives to open a small grocery shop in Fochabers, in the heart of an area famed for its fruit, vegetables, grouse, and deer.

George's wife, Margaret, found time from the busy toil of shop life to make her own jams and jellies, which soon found a ready market at Gordon Castle.

Other prestigious markets soon opened up, and the family business grew from strength to strength, taking George Baxter's proud motto of 'be different, be better' as its inspiration.

George and Margaret's son, William, married in 1914 and he and his wife, Ethel, built a factory beside the Spey to meet the burgeoning demand for their products.

As William Baxter traversed the country marketing his wares, Ethel hit upon the product that has since become something of a Baxter 'trademark' - the famed Royal Game Soup.

Other ranges of soups and jams followed over the years and the Baxters Food Group, which now enjoys worldwide sales, has also in recent years bought over other food groups.

While generations of Baxters have flourished peacefully in Fife and Morayshire, separate families of Baxters much further west became embroiled in some of the bloodiest episodes in Scotland's turbulent history – and this was through their kinship with Clan MacMillan.

One account of this kinship with the proud MacMillans relates to an Archibald Baan MacMillan of Knapdale, in Argyll, who had quarrelled with a prominent neighbour and, in the heat of the moment, slew him.

Fleeing for his life, pursued by his victim's kinsfolk, a breathless MacMillan found refuge in the kitchens of a residence of the Campbells of Argyll, where a sympathetic cook, who had been baking at the time, agreed to change clothes with him.

The ruse worked, and MacMillan is reputed to have from that point on assumed the name of MacBhaxter ('son of the baxter', or baker). His descendants, who eventually settled in Cowal, in Argyll, carried on the name.

This incident is reckoned by some sources to have occurred in the latter decades of the fifteenth century, but a record from 1377 indicates the Baxters were probably considered a sept, or branch, of the MacMillans, from a much earlier date.

As kinsfolk of the MacMillans, the Baxters shared not only in the clan's fortunes, but also in their misfortunes.

Chapter three:

Battleaxe and broadsword

A hand brandishing a sword is the crest and 'I learn to succour the distressed', is the motto of Clan MacMillan, the name deriving from the Gaelic 'Mhaolian', meaning 'tonsured', and this indicates that the ancestors of the clan were a family of priests who, in all probability, traced their origins back to Ireland.

Whatever their origins, these 'sons of the tonsured', or MacMillans, are recorded in the twelfth century as settled in lands beside Loch Arkaig, in Lochaber, and later in territory near Loch Tay.

Much of Argyll was held under the powerful sway of the MacDonald Lords of the Isles, who in 1360 confirmed a Malcolm Mor MacMillan in his ownership of lands in Knapdale, in mid-Argyll, and it was here that the

MacMillan stronghold of Castle Sween was built, in the heart of the territory that had been settled by the MacBhaxters.

A grandson of Malcolm, known to posterity as Lachlan MacMillan of Knap, was slain with hundreds of his clansmen and kinsmen such as the MacBhaxters (who would later adopt the more familiar English spelling of Baxter), in one of the most ferocious clan battles ever fought on Scottish soil.

Known as the battle of Harlaw, or the battle of Red Harlaw, it was fought on July 24, 1411, and was basically a bloody showdown between the wild an unruly clansmen of the west and north of Scotland and their rather more law-abiding neighbours in the lowlands and the northeast.

Donald MacDonald, 2nd Lord of the Isles, had mustered about 6,000 of his most battle-hardened clansmen and kinsmen such as the MacMillans - and their kinsmen such as the MacBhaxters - and torched the town of Inverness after having crossed to the mainland from the MacDonald stronghold of Ardtornish, on the

Sound of Mull, and marching up the Great Glen.

His already formidable strength swelled to 10,000 after other clans (including Chattan, Cameron, Macintosh, and MacLeod) joined him on his destructive progress and, promising them rich plunder, he marched them towards Inverness, where the citizens cowered in terror.

The Earl of Mar, however, hastily assembled a force of northeast lairds and their kinsfolk, while the provost of Aberdeen also raised a citizen militia.

The opposing forces finally met just north of Aberdeen, and battle was joined shortly after the summer sun had risen in the east.

The fearless clansmen repeatedly charged the ranks of Mar's forces, only to be cut down like ripe corn, but not before they had exacted their own dreadful toll in blood.

As the sun sank low in the west, both sides were totally exhausted and had to retire from the carnage, leaving behind a battlefield littered with the bodies of at least 1,000 clansmen and 600 of Mar's men.

Aberdeen had been saved, but at a terrible cost to both sides.

In 1396, a contingent of MacMillans were wiped out in the infamous Battle of the Clans that took place on a large, flat meadow on the outskirts of Perth known as the North Inch.

A bitter feud had dragged out for some time between Clan Kay and the great confederation of clans known as Clan Chattan - a bloody vendetta that had not only visited mayhem on the clans themselves, but also blighted the lives of their more peaceful neighbours.

The MacMillans and their MacBhaxter kinsfolk had been embroiled in a feud for the captaincy of the Chattan confederation, and found themselves on the side of Clan Kay and their supporters.

In a desperate bid to resolve the vendetta, the monarch, Robert III, arranged for a gladiatorial combat between the two warring factions, watched by not only the king himself but a glittering array of courtiers and even the Dauphin of France.

Sixty champions were chosen from each side and, armed with a deadly arsenal of broadswords, dirks, and battleaxes, and allowed to shoot off one volley of crossbow bolts, the 120 warriors battled it out until only eleven Chattans were left standing on the blood-soaked field of combat.

The sole Kay survivor took to his heels and swam for safety across the River Tay.

As one of the clans that made up the confederacy of clans who owed allegiance to the MacDonald Lords of the Isles, the fortunes of the MacMillans and their MacBhaxter kinsfolk were inextricably linked to those of the MacDonalds.

This was to have dire consequences for the MacMillans and other members of the confederation when, in 1493, with royal authority being flouted at every turn, an exasperated James IV finally annexed the Lordship of the Isles to the Crown.

The resultant power vacuum led to virtual anarchy, with powerful clans such as the Campbells encroaching on territory held by less powerful clans such as the MacMillans and their kinsfolk.

Some MacMillans and kinsfolk such as the MacBhaxters found a new home much further southwest, in Galloway, while others were forced to flee from Knapdale into Lochaber, where they found themselves tenants of the Macintoshes, who in turn owed allegiance to Clan Cameron.

Any Baxters of today who can trace ancestry back to those areas of Argyll held by the MacMillans are entitled to claim kinship with the clan and adopt the MacMillan, crest, motto, and tartan.

Many of those MacMillans and their Baxter kinsfolk who later found a home in Galloway played a leading role in the bitter seventeenth century struggles between Crown and Covenant.

One of the most prominent of these Covenanters was the Reverend John MacMillan, who as late as 1703 was deposed from his practice for his continued opposition to authority.

The Covenanters had taken their name from the National Covenant, first signed in the Greyfriars Kirkyard in Edinburgh in February of 1638 in defence of the Presbyterian religion and in opposition to the king's claim of supremacy in matters of religion.

During the Killing Time of 1684 to 1685, hundreds of Covenanters in the southwest of Scotland, such as the MacMillans and their Baxter kinsfolk, paid dearly for their uncompromising adherence to their faith and their opposition to the Stuart kings.

Another strict adherent of the Protestant faith was Richard Baxter, a leader of the Puritan Church in England.

Born in Shropshire in 1615, Baxter gained a formidable reputation in his lifetime as not only a fiery preacher but as a scholar, and became known as 'the chief of English Protestant Schoolmen.'

Also the author of a number of theological works, he was imprisoned for a time following the Restoration of Charles II in 1660, because of his uncompromising religious stance.

Chapter four:

On the world stage

Far from civil war and strife, Baxters have gained celebrity in fields that include literature, acting, and sport.

James Keir Baxter, whose maternal grandfather was Scottish, was the New Zealand poet known as 'The Tribal Prophet', and who was born in South Dunedin in 1926. He died in 1972.

He strongly identified himself with New Zealand's indigenous Maori culture, to the extent that he adopted the Maori form of his name, Hemi, in 1969, and moved to the Maori settlement of Jerusalem, on the Wanganui River.

Baxter was also the author in 1945 of the critically acclaimed *Beyond the Pallisades*.

In contemporary times, Stephen Baxter, born in Liverpool in 1957, is the acclaimed science fiction author with degrees in both mathematics and engineering and who is best known for his *Xeelee Sequence* of tales.

On the stage, Anne Baxter, who was born in Michigan City, Indiana, in 1923, was the American actress who won an Oscar for Best Supporting Actress for the 1946 film *The Razor's Edge*.

She also played a memorable role as the Egyptian princess Nefertiti in the 1956 Cecil B. DeMille epic *The Ten Commandments*, while she starred shortly before her death in 1985 in the American television series *Hotel*.

Baxter, who has a star on the Hollywood Walk of Fame, was a maternal granddaughter of the famous American architect Frank Lloyd Wright.

Also on the stage, Warner Baxter, born in Columbus, Ohio, and who died in 1951, began his career in vaudeville, while his first starring role in film was as the Cisco Kid in the 1929 *Old Arizona*, for which he won an Oscar for Best Actor.

By 1930, he was the highest paid actor in Hollywood, and he also has a star on the Hollywood Walk of Fame.

Warner Baxter seems to have led something of a charmed life because, when he was aged nine the family moved from Ohio to San Francisco – where they narrowly escaped death in the great 1906 San Francisco earthquake!

Meredith Baxter, born in South Pasadena, California, in 1947, is a popular American television actress who took her stage name from her mother's maiden name.

Her mother, Meredith Blake, also an actress, was the creator of a number of American sitcoms.

In the world of broadcasting, Biddy Baxter is the British television producer best known for her work with the children's magazine show *Blue Peter*.

Awarded an MBE in 1981, she is also a fellow of the Royal Television Society.

Raymond Baxter, born in 1922, is a distinguished British television presenter and writer best known as being the first presenter of the BBC's futuristic *Tomorrow's World* series.

Serving with the Royal Air Force during the Second World War, he was mentioned in dispatches for his role in the bombing in March of

1945 of the German headquarters for the V1 and V2 rocket programme.

In the world of comedy, Stanley Baxter is the multi-talented comic actor and impressionist who is probably best known for the 'Parliamo Glasgow' routines that featured on his hugely popular television shows.

Born in Glasgow in 1926, Baxter's first taste of the stage was when he entertained troops during National Service.

He then worked for three years at Glasgow's Citizen's Theatre, before moving to London in 1959 and subsequently launching his television career.

Until his retiral in 1991, Baxter was also a popular star of pantomime.

On the football pitch, Jim Baxter is a legendary hero of the game in Scotland, and is fondly remembered for his role in Scotland's 3-2 defeat of England at Wembley Stadium in 1967.

Scotland's victory had made them the first team to beat England after they had won the 1966 World Cup, and Baxter had treated the tartan-clad Scottish fans to a virtuoso performance as he cheekily taunted the opposition with a classic display of 'keepie-uppie'.

Born in Hill O' Beath, in Fife, in 1939, 'Slim Jim' Baxter began his playing career with Raith Rovers, later moving to Glasgow Rangers in 1960.

After five years with Rangers, he played for a time with Sunderland before joining Nottingham Forest in 1967. He returned to Rangers for a brief spell in 1969, but he retired from the game in 1970.

In many ways a flawed footballing genius, Baxter became infamous for his drinking and gambling exploits and died in 2001.

In the world of contemporary music, Jeff 'Skunk' Baxter is the legendary American rock guitarist, born in Washington, D.C. in 1948, and best known for his work with the Doobie Brothers and Steely Dan.

'Baxter' is also the name of a county in the American state of Arkansas, and a city in Crow Wing County, Arizona.

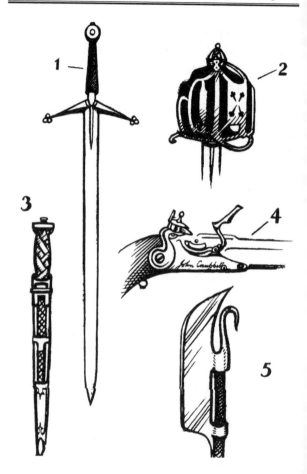

Highland weapons

1)   The claymore or two-handed sword
        (fifteenth or early sixteenth century)

2)   Basket hilt of broadsword
        made in Stirling, 1716

3)   Highland dirk
        (eighteenth century)

4)   Steel pistol *(detail)* made in Doune

5)   Head of Lochaber Axe as carried
        in the '45 and earlier